W9-BKW-242

Jean Genet in Tangier

Translated by Paul Bowles
Introduction by William Burroughs

JEAN GENET
IN TANGIER

MOHAMED CHOUKRI

The Ecco Press   New York

Copyright © 1973, 1974 by Paul Bowles
All rights reserved
First published in 1974 by The Ecco Press
1 West 30th Street, New York, N.Y. 10001
Published simultaneously in Canada by
The Macmillan Company of Canada Limited
SBN 912-94608-3
Library of Congress catalog card number: 73-86613
Printed in U.S.A.
Designed by Ronald Gordon

FOREWORD

It is my feeling that Choukri's book on Genet in
Tangier needs no introduction. It is a full-length
portrait of Jean Genet. Anyone who reads it will see
Genet as clearly as I saw him in Chicago. To select
a few quotes:

"The police have never been human, and the day
they become human they'll no longer be police."
Exactly. Some police are admittedly better than
others, as a cold is better to catch than rabies. But
who wants either?

"There's no absolute no and no absolute yes.
I'm sitting here with you now, but I might easily
not be." It was purely a matter of luck that landed
Genet in Chicago in 1968 (when he covered the
Democratic Convention for *Esquire*).

"I'm neither Existentialist nor Absurdist. I don't
believe in such classifications. I'm only a writer,
either a good one or a bad one." I have been equally
impatient of such classifications. Am I a Beat

writer? a black humorist? and so on. There is good writing and bad writing. Giving names is meaningless.

"I've always been writing, even before I ever tried to write anything. The career of a writer doesn't begin at the moment he begins to write. The career and the writing may coincide earlier or later." I did not start to write until the age of thirty-five. In an essay on Kerouac, written before I had seen Choukri's notes, I said exactly the same thing: "I was always writing, long before I actually wrote anything." This shared conviction made it possible for Jean Genet and me to communicate in Chicago despite my atrocious French and his non-existent English. Had he considered himself an Existentialist or an Absurdist, communication would have been impossible.

As I read Choukri's notes, I saw and heard Jean Genet as clearly as if I had been watching a film of him. To achieve such precision simply by reporting what happened and what was said, one must have a rare clarity of vision. Choukri is a writer.

—William Burroughs

Jean Genet in Tangier

18 / XI / 68

I was sitting in the Café Central with Gerard Beatty. Suddenly he said: Look! That's Jean Genet!

He walks slowly, his hands in his pockets, unkempt. He stares fixedly at the terrace of the Café Central.

He stood still, turned completely around, and looked in the direction of the Café Fuentes. Then he chose the Café Tanger. I said to Gerard: I've got to meet him.

No! Don't even try.

Why not?

He goes into his shell and stays there. You can't make contact with him. At least that's what I'm told.

I decided to disregard Gerard's warning. I could see Genet over at the Café Tanger, sitting down beside a young Moroccan.

We sat on for nearly an hour, listing the painters and writers who have visited Tangier over the years. One eye on the human ants milling in the square, and the other on Jean Genet's head, glistening in the sunlight. I saw him start to get up. It was about three o'clock. I said to Gerard: Watch carefully, now.

Gerard cried: You're out of your mind! I turned to him and grinned.

Behind me, I heard him objecting: What you're doing is insane!

He was walking. I went slowly toward him. He stopped, his hands in his pockets, leaned forward slightly.

He looked searchingly at me. I said: You *are* Monsieur Genet, aren't you?

He hesitated for an instant, and without replying, said: Who are you?

I waited before saying: A Moroccan writer.

He held out his hand. *Enchanté.*

I saw Gerard watching me from behind the café window, surprised and smiling.

As we walked up the Siaghines I asked Genet if he liked Tangier.

Ça va, he said noncommittally.

Don't you think it's one of the most beautiful cities in the world?

Certainly not! Whatever gave you such an idea?

I'd heard it was, I said.

It's not true. In Asia there are cities far more beautiful.

During the twenty minutes it took us to walk from the Zoco Chico to the Hotel Minzah, we talked about Moroccan writers, and about some of the problems they must confront both in their writing and in the publication of it. When we were in front of the hotel he gave me his hand, saying: I always take a nap. Tomorrow, if you like, we can meet in the Zoco Chico. Around two in the afternoon?

19 / XI / 68

I sat down in the Café el Menara. I was thinking: Will he come or not? For me it was still the previous day because what I was waiting for had not yet happened.

I saw him coming along, slowly, as before. I waved to him. His eyes lighted up and he smiled. I rose. We shook hands warmly.

His expression is more friendly than yesterday. We sat down. He ordered a glass of mint tea, and I took a second one. Some of the passers-by go up or down the street and do not return. Others walk back and forth constantly. Most of these are youths and boys looking for tourists.

I don't understand why they haven't translated any of your books into Arabic, I said.

You mean the Arabic of the Koran?

I explained that Koranic Arabic is Classical Arabic.

I don't know. No one has asked to do it. Maybe

some day they will, maybe not. It depends on whether my things interest them at that point. Personally, I think the Arabs are extremely sensitive when it comes to questions of morality.

I had with me a copy of *Le Rouge et le noir*. He riffled the pages. Do you like this?

Yes. I read it first in Arabic. Now I'm rereading it in French. And I added: Julien's family life is like my own in some ways. One thing in particular is almost identical: Monsieur Sorel bound out his son Julien to the mayor of the town for three hundred francs a year, and my father rented me for thirty pesetas a month to a hashish-smoker who ran a café in the quarter of Ain Khabbaz where we lived in Tetuán.

I see your trouble. And you're not the only one. You'll never find beauty in literature that way. You shouldn't read with that sort of thing in mind, with the idea that the life of one or another protagonist has something to do with your own life. You have to keep things separate. Your life is nobody else's life.

I thought of the personality of Basil (in *The Picture of Dorian Gray*) and his conversation with

Lord Henry on the subject of art and its relation to the personal life of the artist.

What I meant was that Julien makes me see my own past in a different light, and that consoles me for the present, I told him.

Maintenant je comprends, he said. Julien's life is marvelous. He's real. Stendhal was one of the great writers of his time.

Meursault refusing to defend himself (in Camus's *L'Etranger*) reminds me of Julien in prison.

It's not the same thing, he said. And he began to speak at some length about the era in which Stendhal wrote. Then he said: But Camus was luckier. *L'Etranger* was written in an age when France was no longer run by the army and the church. The hero of today's books is more free to refuse. It's very rare that he dies for the woman he loves. She may shoot at him, but he won't feel any love for her in his cell, or repeat her name on his way to the guillotine. You could say that Kafka was the first to write about the *refus obscur*. Take K. in *The Trial*, for instance. The charges against him are grave. He must cooperate, but he has no trial. At the moment when his life is in danger, he's playing the comic lover with a woman.

After a moment I asked him about his friend Sartre. I haven't seen him in two years, he said.

I've read most of his books. I'd like to talk with him some day.

That's easy to arrange. Then he added: Postwar Sartre is not prewar Sartre. He came out of his German prison with a new skin. So did I. If we hadn't both changed our skins we wouldn't have been friends.

I walked with him to the hotel. On the way I asked him if he spoke Spanish.

No, he said. I was in Chicago in August. I learned a few words there.

And English?

Non plus.

I said goodbye to him in front of the hotel without making a new appointment.

20 / XI / 68

He was walking in the Medina with Brion Gysin,
coming up from the Calle Bencharqi. Without
greeting me, he launched into an explanation of the
color red in Stendhal's novel. Listen! Red doesn't
mean the army, in spite of what I told you yesterday. It stands for the judges who wore red capes.
Red for the judges and black for the priests.

21 / XI / 68

I met him in the Zoco Chico some time after mid-day. We talked for an hour. He asked me questions about Morocco, from the point of view of its culture and economy. He wanted to know whether professors and students mingled during the hours of recreation or outside school.

No. Neither the Moroccans nor the French. There's a high screen between the teacher and the pupil here.

But why?

I don't know.

He seemed disappointed. Soon we began to talk about Islam and Christianity, about what the four evangelists wrote, and the revealing of the Koran.

Personally, I believe the Koran is more trust-worthy than Matthew, Mark, Luke, and John, he said.

We were silent for a moment. Then we began a

new conversation. Have you read anything by any Arab writers? I asked him.

Unfortunately not. Only a few things by Katib Yacine. He's a friend of mine.

To be certain, I went on: Not even Taha Hussein? Or Tawfiq el-Hakim?

Who are they?

Two Egyptian writers. Some of their books are translated into French, and other languages. Especially Tawfiq el-Hakim.

I don't know them. Some day I hope to read them.

24 / IX / 69

This morning Gerard Beatty told me he had seen Jean Genet in the Zoco Chico. In the afternoon I ran into Brion Gysin at the Café Zagora. His mangled foot was still bad enough to keep him from walking. He asked me to go to the Hotel Minzah and deliver an invitation to Genet for a lunch he is giving tomorrow noon.

I spoke on a house telephone with him from the lobby. He accepted the invitation immediately, and went on to ask me if I had read *La Chartreuse de Parme*. I felt ill at ease, and laughed before I answered: Oh, no. Not yet. But I'm surely going to read it very soon.

I advised you last year to read it, he said. Forgive me if I don't come downstairs. I've taken some Nembutal pills. *A demain, chez l'Américain.*

Brion was waiting for me at the Café Zagora. I went with him to his apartment. On the way he began to complain about his foot, and about certain friends who would not let him work at the new book he was trying to write. We stopped into the Parade Bar. Brion ordered a whiskey, and I had a beer. He insisted it was the evil eye of Princess Ruspoli which had caused the motorcycle accident that had ruined his foot.

I can still see that last look she gave John and me before we got on to the motorcycle. There's no doubt in my mind. She practices magic.

It seems Genet's back in town, I said to Brion.

Yes, he said. And that Nembutal's going to kill him unless he goes into a nursing home and gets treatment.

It's several years since he's written anything, I said.

I don't think he's going to write anything more, Brion said. He feels that he's done what he had to do.

He went on to say that he had been rereading some of the books. I can't believe that man didn't have a classical education, he said. There's some mystery that he's trying to hide. His life is one of the great literary mysteries of the century.

I asked him how he thought it was possible for

Genet to have had such an education. He said he
had spoken of it with him, but Genet would never
say more than that his entire education came from
the thieves and vagabonds he happened to know
in his formative years. Brion told him outright that
he wasn't going to accept that, and added that he
suspected he'd been brought up in a Catholic in-
stitution.

You don't learn the language of Racine in the
street, Brion went on. And I wouldn't be surprised
if Genet knew Greek and Latin.

I asked him how Genet had reacted to that.

No reaction, except that he got a bit pale, and
looked very much astonished. Then he laughed and
denied it. And he went through the same story as
always. The thieves and the pimps. He claims it
was a very special period that didn't last, the time
when the criminals all spoke perfect French! No.
You've got Genet the genius, and Genet the criminal. But there's another Genet, Genet the third,
Genet the mystery man.

25 / IX / 69

We ate out of the pot with our hands. Genet scarcely touched the food. After lunch H. stirred things up by introducing the subject of religion. Genet seemed interested in the Koran. Then H. asked Genet why he stayed at the Minzah if he liked the company of the poorer Moroccans. Genet laughed.

Don't you know why?

No.

Because I'm a dirty dog. I stay at the Minzah or the Hilton because I like to see elegant people waiting on a filthy cur like me.

We all laughed. H. said: And why should you be a filthy cur?

Because that's what they think I am.

Brion was still very much upset about his foot. I had with me *L'Etre et le néant, La Chartreuse de Parme,* and *Le Balcon.* Genet picked up the Stendhal: Sartre is my friend, but *La Chartreuse de Parme* is a better book than *L'Etre et le néant.*

Sartre's book is too complicated, I said. In three

years I've only been able to read a hundred and thirty pages. Sometimes one single sentence has sent me off to read a whole book.

I had trouble with it myself the first time I read it, Genet told me. One day I took the book with me to Sartre's house, and I said to him: This book of yours is difficult. He took it out of my hand and began to write notes and numbers in it, to show me the sequence in which I ought to read the various parts. And he said: I think now you'll be able to understand it without any trouble. He was right. I *could* understand it, using the method he worked out for me.

And why didn't he write it in the order he showed you, then? I asked.

He wrote it for specialists. At least, that's what he told me.

Then H. asked Genet: Do you believe God exists?

Genet laughed. I don't know. All I know is that the world exists. But only God himself knows whether He exists.

The philosophers are right, H. said. God doesn't exist.

Genet said jokingly: So you're an atheist.

Brion's cook interrupted. H. is always like this. But he can't explain why he's an atheist. He talks like this only when he's with foreigners. When he's with Moslems he's a hypocrite and a coward. Because he knows God does exist.

And you? cried H. Can you explain your faith?

Yes. God exists. That's enough.

God doesn't exist. That too is enough.

I asked Genet to inscribe *Le Balcon* for me. He wrote the dedication in both Arabic and French.

We left the lunch table about half past five, and said goodbye to Genet in the Place de France. There we met two girls. H. knew one of them, and so we went to his apartment to drink wine and smoke kif. During the night a commotion woke me up. H.'s girl came into my room crying, and sat down near me half naked, to complain about how rough men are. H. followed her in, and persuaded her to go back into his room with him. Then I noticed that the girl who lay beside me was also weeping. I could not bring myself to ask her why.

From far away in the night came the music of a wedding. Distant sounds of festivity always depress me. I thought: man is very fragile.

26 / IX / 69

Today I met him at the Café el Menara. I had *The Idiot* and some magazines in Arabic under my arm: *al-Adab, Maouaqif,* and *al-Maarifa.* He remarked that from what he had read on the subject by non-Arab writers, Arabic literature did not concern itself with general problems, but was predicated solely upon Arab sentiment.

The humanity that lies beyond its frontiers does not interest it much.

I said: Some Arab critics consider you an Existentialist, and others say you belong to the school of the Absurd.

He looked at me, startled. Who wrote such stuff about me?

Some Arab critics.

They're wrong, whoever they are. I'm neither Existentialist nor Absurdist. I don't believe in such classifications. I'm only a writer, either a good one or a bad one.

A boy came to the table. Genet shook his hand eagerly. He turned to me: He's a friend of mine. I met him last year.

The two exchanged knowing glances, but said nothing to each other. When he did speak to the boy, Genet used a mixture of Moroccan and Tunisian Arabic. The boy laughed. Genet pointed to the worn-out shoes he was wearing, and said: How much would a new pair of shoes cost?

The boy murmured: A thousand francs.

Is that all? said Genet. The boy nodded, and he gave him fifteen hundred francs with the warning: If you don't go and buy some new shoes you and I are no longer friends. I won't speak to you if I see you.

The boy smiled and ran off.

Genet turned to me. He's a bright boy. Why isn't he in school?

I explained.

I understand, he said.

After a moment I asked him if he agreed with what Sartre had written about him in his book.

Without hesitating he replied: Naturally I agree. Sartre read me the first hundred pages aloud, and then asked me if I thought it was all right as it was, and if he should go on or not.

Some people seem to think he was more interested in expounding a few of his own favorite themes there than he was in the books he was writing about. The same thing they say about his book on Baudelaire.

I disagree, he said. If Sartre hadn't been interested above all in my books he couldn't have written the book he wrote. He knows what I've written from having studied it, and he knows my personal life from the fact that we're friends. He used that knowledge to form his ideas about me.

After a moment I said: Brion tells me that Claudel, the writer's son, is planning to have an official reception for you at the French Consulate.

I shan't accept. I never go to things like that. The Cuban Consul in Paris invited me for a holiday in Cuba. Fidel Castro is a friend of mine, but I don't accept any official invitations from him. The only head of state I've sat at table with is Pompidou, and that was because he had allowed certain friends of mine who had been exiled to return to France. I hate all governments. I'm not welcome in the

United States, for instance, because of my homosexuality and because of my criminal record. As if there were no ex-convicts or homosexuals in the United States! And I can't go to the Soviet Union because Zhdanov, under Stalin, forbade all my works there.

He picked up my Arabic version of *The Idiot*. Who wrote this? he asked. I told him what the book was.

I like *The Brothers Karamazov* better, he said.

Brion thinks *The Idiot* is better, I told him.

And you?

I'm just starting it. But I admire *The Brothers Karamazov*.

Later I caught sight of him in the Zoco de Fuera, with a tall, husky Moroccan whom I know slightly. I was going up from the Zoco Chico to the Boulevard, and they were walking toward Sidi Bouabid. Seeing them going alone together in the crowd made me think of *Le Journal du voleur*. He walked with his friend Stilitano like that in the barrios of Barcelona. At home I looked for the passage. *Mes vêtements étaient sales et pitoyables. J'avais faim et froid. Voici l'époque de ma vie la plus misérable.*

(Some months later I met the Moroccan and asked him if he had heard from Genet. Oh, that rich Frenchman? He told me he was going to send me a little money, but he hasn't sent anything. Those people, once they go away, they never think of you again.)

27 / IX / 69

We were approaching his hotel. I asked him if he had read anything by Tennessee Williams.

No, and I don't want to read anything, either.

Why not?

Everything I've read about his works leads me to think it wouldn't interest me.

Don't you know him personally? I asked him.

He telephoned me once in Paris. I wasn't very well at the time. We made an appointment for the next day, but I was too ill to keep it.

I saw Gerard Beatty coming toward us.

I introduced him to Genet, and he began to enthuse about *Le Journal du voleur*. Then they got onto Tangier and the people in it. Suddenly Gerard said: Even the police are human here. Yesterday they took me to the comisaria because I didn't have my passport with me. But after a few minutes they let me go. They're human.

Genet, who had been visibly critical from the

beginning of the anecdote, burst out: Listen to me! You're being offensive. If you've read my books, you know my low opinion of the police. In spite of that, you can stand there and tell me how human they are. The police have never been human, and the day they become human they'll no longer be police.

I'm sorry, Gerard said. I wasn't thinking in that way. I only meant——

Genet had said a quick goodbye and gone into the hotel.

28 / IX / 69

At the Brasserie de France. Abdeslam, a friend of Edouard Roditi's, came up to our table, sat down beside me, and began to whisper in my ear. Isn't that the famous French writer? I want to talk to him. Will you interpret for me?

It looked as though he were going to ask him for money, and I was uncomfortable. I asked him what he wanted to talk to him about. About a big project, he whispered. I want him to help me finish it.

It still sounded like money to me, so I told him Genet spoke Arabic and he could talk to him himself.

Kif entaya, mossieu? he said to Genet.

Labess. Genet smiled and looked at me inquiringly.

A friend of mine, I had to say.

Abdeslam still wanted me to interpret. I'm making a book, and I want him to write a long poem for it. Very long. I'll put it in the front of the book so everyone will see it.

I translated for Genet.

What should be the subject of this long poem? he asked.

I want a poem about Tangier, Abdeslam said.

Genet smiled again. Tell him I'm here working for Gallimard, my publisher. Tell him I've signed a contract and accepted an advance to write a book, so I can't write any poems for him, either long or short.

If Genet had not continued to speak with perfect seriousness through this nonsense, I should have burst out laughing. Abdeslam can scarcely sign his name legibly in Arabic. Probably Edouard Roditi once told him that papers in the handwriting of famous authors are worth money, and he already had a prospective customer in mind for Genet's poem. Abdeslam persisted. Tell him if he can't write it now he can write it later in Paris and send it to me.

A crippled boy came to our table, and Genet handed him a thousand-franc note, Abdeslam watching every move. Then a dwarf named Mokhtar, who had been standing outside, burst in and rushed to the table with his hand out. Genet had nothing to give him, so he told him to share with his friend the cripple. This brought on a fight between the dwarf and the cripple, right in the middle of the café. To stop it, Genet called the waiter and asked him to lend him five hundred francs. Give it to the dwarf, he told me, and he paid the bill.

When he and I were in the street, Genet said to me: Who was that character?

The one who wanted a poem? He's a parachutist, I told him. But he deserted or was discharged.

What's he doing here in Tangier? he wanted to know.

I thought of telling him the truth, which was that he earned his living by going to bed with tourists, but I remembered that Genet too had done the same thing when he was young. So I said: He doesn't do anything. There's a French writer who sends him money every month.

You mean to say that Morocco's security is in the hands of creatures like that? He wouldn't even be able to wash the dishes in the kitchen.

29 / IX / 69—A.M.

I saw him coming in our direction, and I said to my sister: This man coming along here is going to sit down with us.

Who is he?

Papa, I told her, laughing. Once I told him how much Papa hates me, and he offered to be my spiritual father.

She smiled. Poor man! How dirty he is!

We're the poor ones, I said. He's very rich. He's a famous writer.

It's not true! she cried.

Stand up and say hello to him, I told her. He came nearer and glanced at us. Then he smiled at her. As she got up to give him her hand, I said: My sister Malika.

Jean, he said.

How old are you? he asked her.

Fourteen.

Are you sure you're not younger than that?

As if he had offended her, she answered: No! I'm fourteen! He sat down and ordered a whiskey. Looking at her glass of Coca-Cola, he said: And you? Why aren't you drinking whiskey?

I don't drink alcohol. I'm a Moslem.

But some Moslems drink.

Only the disobedient ones, she said.

Mohammed Zerrad arrived. He was a friend of Genet's. We got into a long conversation about which papers were necessary in order to get a passport for the youth.

My sister stood up to go. Genet rose. *Pardon, mademoiselle.*

She's going back to Tetuán, I told him. She was smiling, and trying to withdraw her hand from his grasp.

I'll see you one of these days in Tetuán, he told her in Moghrebi.

When Malika remarked about Genet's unkempt appearance, I was reminded of a passage in *Le Journal du voleur* where he says that it never would have occurred to anyone in the Barrio Chino to wash his clothes. At most you washed your shirt, and then usually only the collar. Looking at him shuffling along today you would have said that he was still observing the same routine. He no longer lives in dirty narrow rooms, or needs a friend like Stilitano who is willing to sleep with the landlady once a week in return for the rent.

Several times he has voiced his enthusiasm for the veil and the djellaba as being the right garments for Moroccan women. *La femme a toujours été un mystère pour l'homme,* he says. It's the fact that she's hidden that makes men curious about her. Is she beautiful or not? Moroccan women look better with their faces covered.

29 / IX / 69—P.M.

I found him waiting for me in front of the hotel entrance. As we went in, I said: Last year they wouldn't let me in here, even though I was invited by an English friend who was staying here.

Why not? he demanded.

Perhaps I wasn't well enough dressed.

That's what I'd imagine. Would you rather go somewhere else?

No! On the contrary. I'll enjoy going with you into a place they've kept me out of.

We sat down in the garden and ordered two whiskeys. There was a young man swimming in the pool in spite of the cold.

He glanced around him nervously, above our heads and under the chairs, saying nothing. I had the impression that he was making certain there were no hidden microphones. Anything is possible, after all, and particularly in the case of a man like Genet.

Good. Let's talk about your writing and publishing problems, he said. I won't give you advice, because no advice that I can give will help decide your future. What I will tell you is that you must choose. Either you stay here as you are, or you go and live somewhere where you can write what you can't write here. I think the Moslems have gone beyond the ethic and traditions of the Koran. But in spite of that, the Koran is still a great book, one that's read by Moslems and non-Moslems alike. You can still read the poems of Baudelaire, Mallarmé, and Rimbaud with great admiration. Why? Because their style goes right on being marvelous.

A moment later he remarked: The situation here is very unstable. Everything reeks of poverty and misery. The foreigners are the only ones here who live like human beings.

30 / IX / 69

We sat down on the terrace of the Café de Paris.
I had Camus's *La Peste* with me.

Do you like this novel? he asked me.

Yes. I'm reading it for the second time.

Are you very fond of Camus?

Yes. I've read a good deal of him.

There was a pause, and I asked him his opinion
of Camus.

He writes like a bull.

I laughed.

Then he went on: I've never liked what he wrote.
Nor did I like his personality. I was never able to
get on with him.

Then you sided with Sartre in their famous con-
troversy?

Naturally. Camus felt more than he thought.

A hippie came up to us and said to Genet in
English: I'm a great admirer of your work. I'm glad
to see you.

Genet looked at me. I translated what the young man had said. They shook hands, and the hippie went off waving and bowing, while Genet smiled. He turned to me and said: The American hippies are wonderful. But their fathers are insupportable.

Abdeslam the parachutist arrived. This time he made a point of sitting down next to Genet and speaking Moghrebi with him. Genet answered in monosyllables. Then Abdeslam turned to me. Tell him he has pretty fingers, he said.

Pretty fingers! I repeated, startled.

Yes, fingers! Tell him his hands are beautiful.

Tell him yourself, if you want to say it. Speak slowly, and he'll understand.

What's he trying to say? Genet asked me a moment later.

He says your fingers are pretty.

Genet stared at his hands with surprise. Then he looked at Abdeslam and burst into laughter. Abdeslam reached out and touched Genet's hand with his fingertips. Then he told him it was a beautiful hand.

Genet turned to me. Ask him what he thinks of my bald head. What does it look like?

Tell him his head is beautiful, too, said Abdeslam. I translated.

Tell him he's crazy, said Genet. It looks like a baboon's ass.

1 / X / 69

We were sitting on the terrace of the Café de Paris.

You seem sad today, I said to him.

I'm always sad, and I always know why, he replied.

I accepted his sadness and did not press him further. I have my own sadnesses.

3 / X / 69

At the Café Zagora.

Did you have a hard time writing your first novel?
I asked him.

No, not very. I wrote the first fifty pages of *Notre
Dame des fleurs* in prison. And when I was trans-
ferred to another jail they somehow got left behind.
I did everything I could to get them back, but it
was hopeless. And so I wrapped myself in my
blanket and rewrote the fifty pages straight off.

I know you didn't start to write until after you
were thirty, I said. Thirty-two or thirty-three.

That's right.

You'd never thought of writing before that?

I've always been writing, even before I ever tried
to write anything. The career of a writer doesn't
begin at the moment he begins to write. The career
and the writing may coincide earlier or later.

You haven't written anything for several years,

have you? Do you consider your literary silence
and your assumption of a political position another
kind of creation, part of your writing?

Literally, I've said what I had to say. Even if
there were anything more to add, I'd keep it to
myself. When I was a convict, the judges had good
reason to keep me in jail. In spite of that, they let
me out. Whether they were afraid to keep me there
any longer, or whether they let me go of their own
free will, I don't know. In any case, the time had
come for me to get out. But I might just as easily still
be in jail.

You mean that sometimes luck wins out over
the law?

Yes, it's possible for it to. There's no absolute
no and no absolute yes. I'm sitting here with you
now, but I might easily not be.

Later he recounted the story of a French painter
who was eating in a restaurant and was asked by
the proprietor to make a drawing of a flower so he
could hang it on the wall of the restaurant. The
painter drew the flower and then told the restau-

rateur how much it was going to cost him. What! the man cried. You dare ask such a price for something that took you five minutes to do?

Not five minutes, forty years, said the painter. Do you want the drawing or don't you?

The restaurateur said: Not at that price. The painter tore up the drawing and continued to eat.

10 / X / 69

At five o'clock we met at the Café Zagora. He asked me what my hunch was: would they give a passport to his friend Mohammed Zerrad, so he could accompany Genet to Paris?

I tried to convince him that bribery was the most practical way to go about trying to get a passport for a young Moroccan who was not in the government and had no contract to work abroad.

That sort of situation doesn't exist in any other country, unless the man is a criminal or a deserter or a spy, he said. They renewed my passport in London in three hours, without making any reference to my career.

That couldn't happen here, I told him. Not yet.

At quarter past five we took a taxi together to the Amalat. There was a long line of people inside, poorly dressed and with anxious faces. A thin man burst out of the office in a state of great excitement. His voice was nervous and hard. Genet turned to me. That's the man who told me to come back at five.

They shut at six, I said.

This official in charge of passports would come out now and then and push those who were waiting. Then he would mouth a few curses and go back inside. Genet was upset. He took a few steps along the corridor, stopped, and muttered: He's an animal, that one. What does he mean, shoving and insulting the people that way? He's a brute!

We waited until all the functionaries had left. All, that is, except those in the passport office. The thin man kept up a steady stream of vituperation against the people waiting. Genet asked me to explain some of the words he was shouting as he went up and down the line. Sometimes he spoke to them in the tone of one who held their very lives in his hands. He pushed one man with particular fury, and literally screamed at him. Again Genet asked for a translation.

He's telling him that as long as he's working in this office he'll never get a passport.

Why not?

Perhaps the bribe wasn't big enough. Sometimes,

if a man argues with him, he locks him up. By the
time he gets to court his fingernails are like claws
and he has a beard down to here.

I told Genet I thought he should try to see the
Governor himself, but he would not even discuss it.
I hate those bureaucratic chiefs, he said.

At the last moment before the building closed,
the thin man spoke to Genet, telling him he could
expedite the passport if all the Moroccan's papers
were in order.

On the way back in the fine rain that blew against
us, he said: What that man wants is a fistful of
banknotes. Isn't that it?

Exactly, I said. You've got it right.

We sat down at the Café de Paris and ordered
two whiskeys. He puffed on a Pantera cigarrillo. I
accepted his invitation to dinner at the Minzah.

The dining room was full of American tourists.
The Moroccan waiters served Genet with great
gusto, treating him as a friend rather than as a man
staying at the hotel, and he never ceased to joke
with them in his halting Arabic. The American
tourists ate, and talked without respite.

Un moment . . . écoutez, said Genet. Can you

hear them? They're chewing on the motors of the planes they wish they were in. In Vietnam, or in the Middle East.

The pianist finished one piece and went into another. I've never heard a pianist quite that bad, Genet said. He plays the way they chew their food and their words.

Genet was happy, but he ate scantily. His only appetities are for alcohol and Nembutal, as he says.

I asked him: What are you reading these days?

If you mean books, I'm not reading anything. All I take with me when I travel is a few clothes and my papers.

You seem to like this hotel.

I know the manager, he said. He's read my books. Sometimes we talk about them, about the ideas behind them. At least in this place I feel at home, and not like just another client.

A Moroccan friend who works at the Minzah has told me a bit about Genet's behavior there. Sometimes he wanders down into the dining room barefoot and in his pajamas, to ask a waiter for a match. He will go back upstairs, and soon reappear to ask for something else. It does not seem to occur to him to use the telephone beside his bed.

After dinner we walked for a half hour on the boulevard. He bought a few newspapers and some magazines, and went back to the hotel.

12 / X / 69

I met him about half past eleven in the morning at the Café de Paris. Mohammed Zerrad was with him. Genet asked us both to have lunch at El Mirador. He is suffering with a kidney ailment, he told me, and called in three different doctors to see him this morning. Each one gave him an injection and then left.

We said goodbye at four o'clock. He had been delightful the entire time. Then he went to take his siesta.

13 / X / 69

I picked him up at the hotel at six this evening, and we went to the Brasserie de France. He was still in pain, and walked very slowly.

14 / X / 69

I met him at the hotel. His health seemed to have improved. He gave me a copy of the Koran in French, saying that he did not fully understand it.

In order to know what most of the commentaries mean, he said, one would have to have studied the history of the Arabs. You've read the book in Arabic, of course? It must be marvelous.

It's the only great work in Arabic, I said.

He began to discuss Mallarmé, for whom I know he has boundless admiration. Among the lines he quoted there was one I particularly liked, and I asked him to write it out for me. Having no paper at hand, he sought out a blank page in the Koran, and wrote: *Et le vide papier que sa blancheur défend.* . . . He was not absolutely certain of his quotation, and he put a question mark after it. (Later when I checked, I discovered that he had written *et* where he should have written *sur*, and *sa* instead of *la*.)

I asked him what, if anything, the name Mallarmé meant in French. He grinned. His name indicates impotence: *mal armé, n'est-ce pas?* Poorly equipped sexually, but with a brain that made up for it.

Then I asked him if *Esquire* had published the complete text of his report on the 1968 Democratic Convention in Chicago. He said they had published only half of it. But I sold the other half to a different magazine, he went on. I know they only buy what I write because it has my signature on it, and not because they want to hear what I have to say about democracy in the United States.

15 / X / 69

Mohammed Zerrad has gone to the country town where he was born, somewhere near Tetuán, to fetch the papers he needs in order to get his passport.

Genet was troubled. Do you think they'll really give him those papers up there in the mountains? Or will it be the same story as it is here when you try to get something from the officials?

But I told you, I said. Everything depends on his personal relationships with the officials themselves or with whoever has contact with them. And if he doesn't know anybody, it can only be solved with money.

Hassan Ouakrim came into the café and sat down with us. It occurred to me that he might be able to help. He knows several functionaries at the Amalat, and never seems to have difficulties getting official papers when he needs them. (Ouakrim runs the Troupe Inoziss, a local dance group.) I introduced him as a friend who might possibly be of use to us. Genet's face showed interest when Ouakrim assured him that he would do everything he could for us, and it showed more interest when he told him he headed a group of dancers. Then he spoke at length of the difficulties of running a project that combined music, dance, and theater. Genet warned him that the artist must be on guard against whatever has influence on his work from the outside. Otherwise, he said, he will constantly be wanting to make it more up to date, which, here in Morocco, means more European. You must keep your music and dance intact, he told Ouakrim.

16 / X / 69

At the Brasserie de France. Mohammed Zerrad has come back from his trip, bringing the necessary papers with him. He says he got them quickly only by paying a good deal of extra money. We congratulated him on his success. We were waiting for Ouakrim to arrive and go with us to the Amalat.

Do you think he can be of any help? Genet asked me.

I think he may. He knows a few people who work there, perhaps because of his dance group.

I see. But is he trustworthy? I mean, can one talk about Moroccan politics in front of him?

I don't think he could do us any harm, I said. All I know about him is that he's always busy with his group. What he wants is to go abroad and study.

When Ouakrim arrived, he took only Zerrad with him to the Amalat. The black waiter came and stood by me. I hear he's a famous writer, he murmured to me.

That's what they say, I told him.

He's a real gentleman, he said.

Genet gave him a friendly smile. The waiter stepped forward and offered him his hand. Speaking in *darija* he said: You are a fine man.

You're a good man too, answered Genet, also in *darija*. Someone called to the waiter, and he left the table.

Aren't you going to ask the French Consul to help you at all? I said. In case you can't get the passport in the ordinary way?

Never, said Genet. That's the one thing I won't do. I'd rather pay any amount of money than have to ask at the French Consulate for anything.

17 / X / 69

I was carrying a copy of *La Peste* with me, having almost finished reading it. We sat down on the terrace of the Café de Paris.

You're still reading that *Peste?* he asked me.

I'm almost to the end.

And my *Balcon?* Have you read that?

Not yet, I said.

Why not?

I'm waiting for the end of the month, so I can buy another copy, I told him.

But what for?

Because my copy's inscribed. You signed it for me.

What's that got to do with it?

I told him I did my reading in cafés, and I was afraid something might happen to the book if I took it out with me. I said I was keeping it as a souvenir.

He reached out and seized my copy of *La Peste*.
Then he ripped out the first page.

Do that with my book, he said. Tear out the
page that has the inscription on it. Read the play.
Then paste the page back in. It's certainly better
to read the book than leave it on the shelf for fear
of losing the signature.

This made me smile. We talked about the price
of books, and I complained that all of his were
too expensive.

I make more money that way, he said.

But why don't they bring out your works in a
cheap edition like Le Livre de Poche, for instance?

I don't know.

But you know that most students can't afford to
buy your books.

It's not my fault, said Genet.

I decided not to say any more.

You told me the last time you were in Tangier
that you hadn't seen Sartre in two years, I said.

That's true. And I still haven't seen him. One
day last year when he was giving a lecture at the
Sorbonne I tried to get in and hear him, but a

girl at the door told me there was no room inside the hall. A lot of other people were trying to get in, but it was impossible.

The girl must have recognized you, I said.

She was a student. I didn't want to insist.

Later, as we were walking along the Boulevard Pasteur, Genet asked if we could go to the bookshop that was the local agency for Gallimard. He had spent the money he had brought with him. I was not certain whether the Librairie des Colonnes was the right one or not, but since we were very near it, I pointed to it and said it might be the one he wanted. We went into the Librairie des Colonnes.

The two ladies who run the bookshop, Madame and Mademoiselle Gérofi, overwhelmed us with courtesy. Genet asked Madame Gérofi if he might speak with her alone for a moment, and she led him up to her office on the balcony. I could see them sitting up there talking. Then Madame Gérofi began to use the typewriter. Brion Gysin says that Genet never uses banks. Gallimard acts as his bank, with the main office in Paris and branches in any bookshop that acts as a Gallimard agency. When he needs money in Paris, he goes to Gallimard to get it, and carries it out with him in a little bag which he hides under his overcoat, at the same time looking around him furtively just as if he had stolen it.

When we were outside in the street again he said: The lady's husband may be able to help with the passport. I've got to meet him in a little while. Let's sit down here and wait. She called him on the phone and he's coming right over.

We went into the Claridge. Once again we began to talk about poetry, through Baudelaire, Verlaine, and Rimbaud. Finally we reached the shrine of Mallarmé, where he had been leading the conversation.

I wish I had *Brise marine* here, he said. I'd like to read it to you.

I said I would run and ask Madame Gérofi for it, and he thought that a good idea.

At the bookshop I found Madame Gérofi very busy with her accounts. I told her Monsieur Genet wanted to see the book. She handed me the poems of Mallarmé. Tell Monsieur Genet that my husband will arrive immediately, she said.

As I was running back to the Claridge I caught

sight of Ouakrim, who said he had been looking for us. At the table he told Genet that he thought there was at least some hope of getting the passport. Genet asked him if he believed Monsieur Gérofi might be of help. It was possible, Ouakrim said, since, being an architect, he had many friends in the government offices.

He can help you if he wants to take the trouble, he told Genet.

Monsieur Gérofi arrived at five o'clock. He is seeing a certain official tomorrow morning and will speak to him.

Ouakrim said that he too had an appointment with someone who might be useful. We got into Monsieur Gérofi's car. Genet still had the borrowed copy of Mallarmé in his hand. He was astonished at the number of difficulties involved in trying to get a simple passport in Morocco. Monsieur Gérofi merely nodded, and said from time to time: That's the way it is here.

We arrived at the Amalat. Ouakrim went in alone while we waited in the car. Genet began to leaf through the Mallarmé volume. If you'll excuse me,

I'm going to read this poem to my friend here, he told Monsieur Gérofi.

Mais je vous en prie, said Monsieur Gérofi.

Genet began to read *Brise marine* in his high, thin voice. When he had finished, he said: Isn't it a miracle, that poem?

We agreed that it was extraordinary. Then he singled out a line that particularly pleased him: *Et la jeune femme allaitant son enfant.*

Ouakrim came back saying that the man he had had the appointment with could not be found. I had noticed that Genet was growing increasingly concerned about getting the passport, and seemed more determined than ever to see it through.

19 / X / 69

I met him around eleven in the morning. We walked down to the Avenida de España and sat at the Puerta del Sol. Genet's friend Georges Lapassade happened by. He seemed perturbed and spoke with great nervousness. I did not particularly like his personality.

In the afternoon I met them both again at the Brasserie de France. We're invited to tea at Madame Gérofi's, Genet told me. You're invited too.

I was tempted to refuse, in order not to have to be near Lapassade, whom I found truly disagreeable. But Monsieur Gérofi arrived then, and we all got into his car. At his apartment we found Emilio Sanz. I had met him at Edouard Rotiti's. He was another whom I found insupportable—the sort of man who waves a flower in the air as he talks, and sniffs it before answering your question or giving what he considers a shattering opinion.

The room encouraged relaxation, and I was tired.

I asked Madame Gérofi if I might have a glass of whiskey instead of tea. The conversation came around to the illustrious persons in the arts and letters who have lived in Tangier. Madame Gérofi spoke of Tennessee Williams, saying that he used to come often, but now had not been here since 1964. The whiskey helped me relax. I drank it slowly. I was practically asleep when I heard Genet exclaim: I've gone into the literary graveyard!

They were talking about the theater. Genet said that it was no longer a viable art form. I asked him what form he thought more valid today.

Something that doesn't yet exist. All the forms used so far have worn out.

Yes. He can say that now that his complete works have been published, I thought. But if he had thought that back in the forties, he wouldn't have written his books, and there would have been only Genet the beggar and thief, Genet condemned to life imprisonment.

As we got up to go, I saw Emilio Sanz take a book from a bookshelf. He handed it to Genet for him to autograph. Genet glanced toward me, asking a question with his eyes. I shrugged slightly, as if I were saying: It's your responsibility. You know how you feel about that sort of man.

I'm sorry, Genet told him. I don't feel well. I can't sign any books today.

Bravo, I thought. What an intuition!

Going down in the elevator Genet asked me: Who is he, the Spaniard with the mustache?

I said he was the son of a banker.

I didn't like him at all, he said.

I don't like him either.

20 / X / 69

I was with Brion at the Brasserie de France. Genet came at about half past six with Mohammed Zerrad. Brion left immediately. We talked for two hours. Mohammed Zerrad also left, and I went with Genet to look for Georges Lapassade in the Zoco Chico. We found him with some Moroccan youths in the Café Central. We went to Maria's restaurant and ordered a bottle of wine. Genet took only one glass. He did not want to eat dinner. Georges and I accompanied him to the hotel, and then I took Lapassade to meet Brion. I talked with them for a half hour or so. While they discussed the old days in Tangier, I fell asleep. When I awoke at two in the morning, they were still talking. I left Lapassade there listening to Brion's discourse on Morocco.

21 / X / 69

Genet, Lapassade, Brion Gysin, and I took a walk through the alleys behind the Zoco Chico. We went into the quarter of Bencharqi. There we found Manolo's house. Inside the door old Alberto the Italian was sitting, watching to see who came in. He brought us some ancient chairs that creaked when we sat in them. The sala was like an icebox. Mildew on the walls. Everything damp and dirty and old. Brion began to talk about the place as it had been in the days of the International Zone.

This city is completely dead, said Lapassade. What's left of it?

I was reminded for some reason of what Genet had written in *Le Journal du voleur*, when he falls asleep leaning against a wall, seeing Tangier in his mind's eye as a *repaire de traîtres*.

The old Italian offered us what remained of a bottle of wine. We thanked him and got up to go.

You can see for yourselves, he said. There's nothing left here. Was it dead like this twenty years ago? In those days there were always five or six clients waiting to get in. Nowadays if we get three during the whole day we're lucky. Sometimes nobody comes in for twenty-four hours straight.

We agreed that the past had been better than the present, and that nothing resembling the past would ever be seen again.

About half past five we went to the Amalat, Genet, Ouakrim, and I. Ouakrim had arranged an appointment with the Governor's private secretary, who gave us a cordial reception. It was the first time during any visit to the Amalat that I had seen a happy expression on Genet's face. The man asked him what sort of work Zerrad would be doing in Paris, and Genet said he would be using him as gardener. I laughed to myself, since he has no garden and no house.

So he will come under the category of servant, the secretary said.

Genet reflected for a moment. *Je vous demande pardon*, he said. I should never think of considering

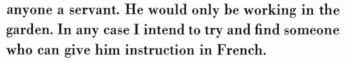

anyone a servant. He would only be working in the garden. In any case I intend to try and find someone who can give him instruction in French.

The man smiled. Apparently he understood Genet's attitude in not wanting to label anyone *servant*. He said he would need a letter from Genet declaring himself financially responsible for Zerrad during his absence from Morocco. The letter would be kept at the Amalat as a guarantee. Genet agreed to take him the letter tomorrow, and the man promised to do everything in his power to see that the document was ready in a day or two. We felt better when we went out into the street. Genet was reflective. He seems to be a civilized man, he said, as if to himself.

22 / X / 69

I met Lapassade, Genet having gone off to take his siesta. We went to Maria's restaurant. As we were eating Lapassade said: It looks to me as if Genet were finished. Where's Genet the adventurer, the Genet of Barcelona, Tunis, Greece?

Lapassade was right, I thought. He was only telling the beads of the past. Whenever I asked him about one of his books, he answered: Oh! I wrote that years ago. One afternoon I said to him: You don't look too well today. He gazed at me with lifeless eyes and said: You're right. I'm very low.

Later at the Brasserie de France. Genet whispered to me, indicating Ouakrim, who sat at the table with us. Does he expect me to pay him for his help?

I put the question to Ouakrim.

Non, monsieur Genet, he said. Then he went into Arabic. We're friends. But you might be able to help me. There's something I'm very much interested in.

Genet said he was ready to help him in whatever way he could.

What he wanted, said Ouakrim, was a letter of introduction to someone in the United States who might be able to get him into a dance school there.

Genet said he would write a letter. We walked to the Minzah and sat in the salon while Genet went up to his room to look for his address book. A letter of introduction from Genet is worth more than a million francs, said Ouakrim.

I agreed that accepting money would have destroyed the friendship. When Genet came back he sat down and wrote two letters, one to Barney Rossett and the other to Richard Seaver, both of Grove Press in New York. I could not help noticing that he ended one of them with the phrase: *Et puis, j'aime tellement les dollars américains!*

23 / X / 69

Mohammed Zerrad got his passport today. Larbi Yacoubi decided to celebrate the occasion by arranging a Gnaoua party for us. It started about eight o'clock. There were Moroccans, both Moslem and Jewish. French, English, and Americans present. The chief of the Gnaoua, black as charcoal, got on friendly terms with Genet during the first rest period between numbers. The music was Sudanese, of course, and the dances expressed basic emotions.

The boy sitting beside me occasionally jumped up and took part in the frantic dancing. From time to time he translated a fragment of the text of a song from the Bambara into Moghrebi, and I re-translated for Genet.

Genet asked the chief how old he was. The old man said: I don't know exactly, but when Kaiser Wilhelm the Second came to Tangier in 1905 I was just beginning to walk.

Genet turned to me: He's handsome, very handsome, that man. Look! He's smoking kif as if he were a young man of twenty!

A photographer among the guests got up and began to take one picture after another. I noticed that Genet seemed delighted to be snapped with the Gnaoua musicians, and annoyed whenever he was caught while talking with a European. For the first time his behavior rather put me off. It seemed to me pretentious, but I accepted it as a part of his personality.

Lapassade smoked kif constantly, moving his head in time with the Sudanese rhythms. The party went on until half past two in the morning. I saw that Genet resented the presence of the Europeans. He kept moving around, changing his seat continually.

When we left, he pulled out a handful of banknotes and put them into the chief's hand. (The musicians already had been paid.) As the money passed between them they exchanged glances. Peace be with you, he said to the black man, who echoed the phrase smiling.

In the street he turned to me, saying: They were wonderful, those Gnaoua, weren't they?

Yes. Personally I don't like Gnaoua parties.

But why not?

They're primitives. I hate everything primitive.

So, what kind of music do you like? he asked me.

Oh, Mozart, Beethoven, Tchaikovsky, Berlioz, people like that.

It seems to me you've been westernized.

Maybe.

Well, I far prefer those Gnaoua we just heard. I used to be like them myself. They're fantastic!

Lapassade turned to me. You simply don't realize their value.

Their value is of no interest to me, I replied. I just don't like them.

Genet told Lapassade: Let him alone. He's free to like what he wants to like.

When we were almost to the Hotel Minzah, Lapassade said to me: I'm going down to the Zoco Chico. Do you want to come along and have some tea?

No, I said curtly. No thanks. I think I'll go to bed.

I said goodnight to Genet and went on my way.

25 / X / 69

Genet and I said our farewells down on the Avenida de España. He was accompanied by Lapassade and a group of French teachers who were up from Rabat on holiday. He and his friend Mohammed Zerrad are setting out today for France via Spain.

I told him that I had left some of the photos taken at the Gnaoua party for him at the hotel. They had not given them to him, but he thanked me, and I walked away.

2 / II / 70

I ran into Mohammed Zerrad in the Zoco de Fuera. We both laughed when we saw each other, even before we spoke. He seemed to be in a good mood. I asked him where Genet was. He did not know, he said. He had been working in Gibraltar for the past month.

I asked him about the trip through Spain. A group of newspaper men came to greet them at the airport, including photographers. He said Genet seemed to know some of them personally, and joked with them as if they were old friends. Then they asked him questions and took down his answers. I asked him if they put any questions to him, too. He said they did, but since he speaks practically no Spanish, he merely said he was a friend. They were taken to someone's house, where they lived a luxurious life during their stay in Madrid. But when they got to Paris, he said, nobody paid any attention to Genet, and this surprised him.

He said they went to a big building full of books, and that Genet told him: This is where I live.

Genet introduced Zerrad to some of the people who were sitting at desks there. Then he asked a girl if she would take his Moroccan friend out in her car, to show him the city. Paris was a fine city, he said, but it was too easy to get lost in. They spent an hour driving around in a beautiful car. It went like a dove, he said. And she was a dove too. A dove driving a dove.

I asked him how they communicated with each other.

Just with smiles, he said. And sometimes we made signs. She was very well educated. You don't have to talk to a girl like that. Afterwards we went back to the book house, and Genet took me to a little hotel and rented a room for me.

It seems that later Genet introduced Zerrad to a French student he was paying for, and the two got into the habit of going out together when Genet was too busy to see either of them. The student lived in the same hotel where Zerrad was staying.

One day Genet came to see Zerrad and handed him some money, saying he was going to a country that was "very far away" to see a production of one of his plays. But as soon as Genet left, the student moved into Zerrad's room. And there was only one bed, he added. But the boy kept saying it would be cheaper.

The student took Zerrad all over Paris with him. Zerrad said he was always afraid they would get separated. The size of the city terrified him. He said the young Frenchman was all right for the first three days, and then he suddenly changed. He began to go into shops and buy things, and Zerrad had to pay for them.

The money was flying out of my pockets! he said. And I'm not Genet. I can't go and get money wherever I happen to be, like him. All I could think of was getting out of there fast while I still had enough to get out with. I kept seeing myself lost in the streets, with my hand out asking for money. So I came back to Tangier and gave my wife the money I had left. Then I went to Gibraltar and got a job the first week.

I said it was strange. Then I asked him what he thought of Genet.

He's a good man, but I don't understand him, he

said. Anyway, he did a lot for me, and I won't forget
it. If it hadn't been for him I'd still be here earning
five or six dirhams a day. That is, if I had work at
all. You can't tell.